T0065681

A
COMMON-SENSE
LOOK
at the
TEN POSITIVE
NOS

JANIS L. TALSMA

WESTBOW
PRESS®
A DIVISION OF THOMAS NELSON
& ZONDERVAN

WestBow Press books may be ordered through booksellers or by contacting:

WestBow Press
A Division of Thomas Nelson & Zondervan
1663 Liberty Drive
Bloomington, IN 47403
www.westbowpress.com
844-714-3454

ISBN: 978-1-6642-8202-5 (sc)
ISBN: 978-1-6642-8203-2 (hc)
ISBN: 978-1-6642-8204-9 (e)

Library of Congress Control Number: 2022919555

Print information available on the last page.

WestBow Press rev. date: 11/09/2022

CONTENTS

I dedicate this book to my children, grandchildren, and great-grandchildren, whom I deeply love and cherish. I want you to know that God is a God of truth so take to heart His wise words for living a good life, and His loving hand of blessing will rest upon you. That is my prayer for each one of you.

Excerpt from 2 Thessalonians 2:15: "Stand firm and hold fast to the teachings we pass on to you."

ACKNOWLEDGMENTS

I have been greatly blessed with many special people who have graciously helped me in a variety of ways in bringing this book to the point of publication. I sincerely thank my friends Reginald Babbey, Pastor Eric Everhart, Pastor Cal Compagner, Pastor Tim Holwerda, and Sharon DeWaal, who, in the early stages of its development, read the draft, made suggestions, and encouraged me to grow this idea. I must also thank my friend Barbara Wiebenga, who so kindly edited my grammar and punctuation, and a huge thank-you to my niece, Melody, who so willingly gave countless hours of her time proofreading and working as a navigator through all the computer functions. I would still be blundering my way through this technological brain if it wasn't for her. And, most of all, I need to acknowledge my ever-patient, always supportive, often stand-in cook, my best friend and the love of my life, my husband, Dutch. Thank you, with all of my heart, for so patiently and lovingly supporting me in an undertaking I have so deeply felt called to accomplish.

PREFACE

The social climate of the latter part of the twentieth and continuing into the twenty-first century is one in which both absolutes and the relevancy and value of the Ten Commandments are being questioned. In view of that, many alternatives have been offered. A *Time* article, written in 2014 by Lex Bayer and John Figdor, "Here's a Secular Alternative to the Ten Commandments," claims that, "Faith in things unseen is becoming less popular to those skeptics who believe in having evidence and who believe that morality is subject to our experience, not by abstract principles or an absolute decree." Other alternatives in this same article suggest that, "Belief in God is not necessary to be a good person, neither is there a right way to live." Shouldn't we then dare ask, "Are there not plenty of wrong ways to live?"

In a *Desert News* 2018 poll, entitled, "Are the Ten Commandments Still Relevant Today?"_Mark Chaves, professor of sociology, religious studies, and divinity at Duke University stated, "American religiosity has been declining for decades and that for a very long time each generation has been a little less religious than the one before." Quotes such as these, plus this one from Hugh Whelchel, executive director for the Institute of Faith, Work, and Economics, which says, "A growing number of millennials say that morals are just what you want them to be," should sound an alarm to our society at large.

My concern is that if absolutes are passé and each person decides for him- or herself what is right and what is wrong, what happens when our opinions clash? What happens when we become a god unto ourselves and do not feel responsible for our behaviors because we can do whatever we feel is OK? What happens when our "OK" behavior brings harm to others? Is it still OK?

It's time, then, to start at the beginning and take a commonsense-but-biblical look at those Ten Commandments. This book is not about judging others or finger-pointing. It's about investigating what these ten words are saying to twenty-first century believers and skeptics alike.

When asked which was the most important commandment, Jesus replied: "Love the Lord your God with all your heart and with all your soul, and with all your mind and with all your strength. This is the first and great commandment. And the second is this: love your neighbor as yourself. There is no commandment greater than these" (Mark 12:30–31).

This is what these Ten Commandments are all about: loving God and our neighbors. In this book, we will see that the first four deal with loving God, and the last six deal with loving our neighbors, or, more broadly, our fellow humans. There are many informative books written on the Ten Commandments. Some of them contain a detailed history of the Israelites as God's specially chosen people. Other books are very theological in nature and delve into a deeper study of these commands. Several years ago, after watching the values and standards of our culture change from having a basic set of norms to the belief that absolutes are archaic and unnecessary, I became deeply worried about what was happening to the heart of our society. Articles that criticized the value and necessity of these Ten Commandments to our twenty-first-century society were becoming more common. It appeared that many people viewed them as negative standards for life by making unreasonable demands of us. Contrary to those beliefs, this author views them as a positive force that delivers a powerful impact for good in our lives. They are all about God's love and concern for us, as well as about meeting the standards of what is right and just. It's all about living a righteous life, which simply means living right, so that it will be good for all, to the end that our relationship with God and our fellow humans will bring blessings and well-being into all lives.

Looking at the title of this book may make one wonder why such a strange name was chosen. Writing a book that speaks plainly and with a commonsense approach appeared to be needed and so, I chose this title. Many struggle with these commands, including skeptics, nominal Christians, as well as practicing Christians. Let's be honest. No one likes to be told what to do. However, we need to understand that our heavenly Father, who passionately loves us, gave us these commandments for our good and well-being. He knows the human heart. If we listen closely to them, we come to realize they are telling us wherein the inclination of our hearts lies.

If it were not so, God would not need to have given them to us.

It would be sad for us if it all ended here. But our loving God knew that because of our rebellious nature, we would not—nor could we—humanly keep these commandments. In His great love, grace, and mercy, He sent the only one who was able to keep all of these Ten Commandments perfectly in our stead. His name is Jesus Christ. The apostle Peter explains it in these words: "He Himself bore our sins in His body on the tree, so that we might die to our sins and live for righteousness; by His wounds you have been healed" (1 Peter 2:24). Those of us who know Christ Jesus as our Savior live by the power of His Spirit and through Him strive to be obedient to God's will for our lives.

Readers, listen to what Moses said to the Israelites. His advice and encouragement apply to us as well. "Acknowledge and take to heart this day that the Lord is God in heaven above and on the earth below. There is no other. Keep his decrees and commands which I am giving you today, so that it may go well with you and your children after you and that you may live long in the land your God gives you for all time" (Deuteronomy 4:30–40).

God Addresses His People

And God spoke all these words: "I am the Lord your God, who brought you out of Egypt, out of the land of slavery" (Exodus 20:2).

As we begin studying the Ten Commandments, we first need to understand that they neither originated out of a vacuum, nor just because there was someone called God who arbitrarily decided He wanted to control peoples' lives. Rather, like most events in history, they were determined to be a necessity and, in this case, began with a people called the Israelites. There were over two million men, women, and children who had just been released from 430 years of slavery in Egypt. They were about to settle and become a community in the land of Canaan. Like other settlements both then and today, laws needed to be established for the common good, health, and safety of all its citizens. Imagine the chaos, harm, and loss of life if civilization lacked civil and moral laws and everyone was permitted to behave as he or she pleased. Even our contemporary civil laws require specific etiquette for drivers, lest they drive their vehicles when, where, and at whatever speeds they feel like. That may be a simplistic example, but we will discover later in this book how even the most basic of laws have a justifiable and wise purpose. So it was with the Israelites too. They needed the wisdom and foreknowledge of the one who knows that at the core of the human heart is self-centeredness.

Having been hundreds of years since the Israelites had been brought into slavery in Egypt, the original captives had long since gone to their graves, and it was their descendants who were released from bondage. Although they knew about this God who freed them and His personal involvement in their history as His people, like their ancestors, they were unfaithful to Him. In reality, they mumbled and grumbled against Him as they made their way through the desert from

Mt. Sinai and on to the promised land of Canaan. Though we certainly wouldn't pretend to know the mind of God as we begin our look at these ten positive nos, it is worth noting that before God gives the very first one, He appears to find it necessary to precede them by getting their attention and reminding them of just who He is and what He has done for them when He states, "I am the Lord your God, who brought you out of Egypt, out of the land of slavery" (Exodus 20:2).

It is important, at the very outset, to understand the use of capitalization of the words *God* and *Lord* within the context of how scripture refers to God in His introduction to the Israelites. Note that they are both capitalized. In that social and religious structure, the capital letter *L* in *Lord*, was a form of address used to indicate one's position of absolute authority—generally, that of master. *God*, with the capital *G*, used by monotheistic religions such as Christianity, used it in recognition of one as supreme ruler. In opposition to that is *god*, spelled with a small *g*, implying that it lacks credibility as a true God and is one fashioned by human imaginings or, in the case of an idol, created by human hands. In view of this, the God who was speaking to the Israelites is making it clear that He is not just some earthly ruler about to give ambiguous human-made orders to His subjects but speaks with absolute authority, surpassing that of all earthly rulers. He is also making it clear that He has chosen them, the descendants of Abraham—the father of the nation of Israel with whom He made a covenant. They were to be His people and He, their God. Furthermore, when He continues this introduction with the words, "Who brought you out of the land of Egypt, out of the land of slavery," He reminds them of the active and caring role he played in their deliverance from bondage. Although one cannot help but wonder why God felt it necessary to introduce Himself in this manner, a short review of what preceded and what was about to follow in the lives of the Israelites gives us a bit of helpful insight.

His Word tells us that, historically, Jacob, grandson of the Old Testament patriarch Abraham, had moved his family to Egypt to survive a great famine in their homeland of Canaan. Over a period of 430 years, the length of time generations of Israelites lived in Egypt, they had multiplied in great numbers and strength to over two million people, with 630,000 of them being able-bodied men. Because of this, a new Pharaoh, who was not familiar with their ancestral history, became fearful they would fight along with Egypt's enemies in times of war. His solution was to enslave them, treating them cruelly and forcing them to become brick makers and field workers. The more they cried for mercy, the more cruelly they were treated. Furthermore, to suppress the number of future Hebrew warriors, the king ordered all newborn sons to be thrown into the Nile River. One of these sons was named Moses. His mother had hidden him in the bulrushes by the river, but he was found by Pharaoh's daughter, who raised him in the royal house and had him educated in Egyptian culture. However, as a grown man, he was called by God to become mediator between Pharaoh, master slave-driver, and the merciful God of the captive Israelites, as well as leader on behalf of these people.

About three months prior to God's reintroduction of Himself to His people at Mt. Sinai, the Israelites had been released from their oppressive bondage. The powerful, dramatic telling of this miraculous escape by the vast multitude of Israelites is recorded in the first fourteen chapters of the book of Exodus. Now, having just escaped from the clutches of Pharaoh's army but not yet a settled community, the Israelites were about to enter foreign lands, whose people were pagans and worshippers of idols. Being the all-knowing God that He is, He knew His chosen people, with their finite minds and proud hearts, would be bent on making their own rules and easily tempted to indulge in the practices of these foreign cultures and their idol worship. In fact, God instructed them to break down those sacred idols of stone into pieces, lest they be tempted to worship them. Sadly, their history shows that time and again, they turned their backs on God to worship those strange, mute, lifeless gods.

As New-Testament believers who look back on the history of the Israelites, it would be easy to wonder why God favored these people and called them His own. We could pose many questions:

- Why did God give the Israelites the ten positive nos, and what was their purpose?
- Are they still relevant to us and the world at large today? Why or why not?
- What happens if we choose to ignore them, make our own rules, or pick and choose those that suit us and discard the rest?
- Do we view them as mere moralistic, binding rules and regulations given by a God who shakes His finger

at us like a scolding parent saying, "No, no, no," to our wants and desires?

- What do these commands reveal about the human character?
- What do they reveal about the character of God, His values, and His expectations for our relationships to one another as well as to Him?

In the following chapters, we will strive to discover answers to these questions as we consider each of God's commandments for His people, one by one. Hear what God says about them in Deuteronomy 5:33: "Walk in all the ways that the Lord your God has commanded you, so that you may live and prosper and prolong your days in the land you will possess." And again, in verse 29, we sense the voice of God as that of a loving Father when He says of the people, "Oh that their hearts would be inclined to fear me and keep my commandments always, so that it might go well with them and their children forever."

Chapter 1

I AM POSITIVELY NUMBER ONE

COMMANDMENT #1

"You shall have no other gods before me" (Exodus 20:3).

I sn't it interesting that God begins these commands by requiring our full and complete allegiance to Him alone? We can't help but wonder why, but when we look at the picture of the Almighty as described in Genesis 1:27, we see Him as our Creator, lovingly at work with His masterpiece of all creation: "So, God created man in His own image, in the image of God He created him; male and female He created them." Furthermore, we are told in Genesis 2:7 that "the Lord God formed man from the dust of the ground and breathed into his nostrils the breath of life and the man became a living being." Our minds can almost picture the Lord forming this person the way an artist works at his sculpture or clay pot, forming it to his liking. We are struck by the vision of this Almighty Creator bending lovingly over this form He has created in His own image and breathing into it His very breath of life. No wonder He says, "You shall have no other gods before me"; it is He who has given us life! Additionally, Ecclesiastes 3:11 states that He, God, "has set eternity in the hearts of men." This tells us that we humans own this sense of time—eternity—beyond our earthly concept of time as well as the existence of someone bigger, greater than ourselves.

It also appears that God and eternity have always been considered part of the same equation—something or someone beyond time as we now know it and beyond ourselves. As a result, people have always sought after that one person or thing—if not God, our Creator, then one of their own creations. The cultures of those foreign lands that the Israelites traveled through on their way to Canaan had gods and goddesses for rain, sun, crops, and fertility: Baal and Asherah being two principal ones, plus a host of others. These were of their own imaginings: inanimate objects made of nothing more than pieces of wood, stone, or metal, sometimes overlaid with gold or silver. They were gods whose power people feared. Oftentimes, fearing they may anger the gods by omission of a sort, the worshippers tried to manipulate and appease them through self-mutilation, prostitution, sexual orgies, drunkenness, and human sacrifices. Sadly, none of this pagan worship would or could bring about a response from these lifeless gods. In addition to all these gods were magicians, sorcerers, and practices of demonic occult activities, such as divination and witchcraft. All these forms of worship were a rebellion against God. In sharp contrast to this, the Israelites had a God who actually spoke to them through Moses in the giving of the Ten Commandments. It seems nearly unbelievable that despite this loving and compassionate God wanting a relationship with them, they built a god—a golden calf—from the melted gold of their wives' and sons' earrings while their living God was giving Moses wise instructions to help them have a good and long life. Paradoxically, they were worshipping this golden calf while God was saying to them, "You shall have no other gods before me." So, what is it about this God that gives Him the right to demand, expect, and deserve such single-minded and wholehearted worship? It was by His authority as a just-and-holy God that He required obedience to these principles for a good, righteous life. Add to that His love for the Israelites, whom He loved as a father loves his children, and who, despite His position of authority, approached them with a desire for a relationship with them as their God.

It was He who saw their misery, heard their cries while under the heavy hand of the Egyptians, and was concerned about their suffering. It was He who chose Moses to act as mediator between Pharaoh and the Israelites to bring about their release from their horrendous plight in Egypt.

In Exodus 6, He is the one who promised to "redeem them with an outstretched arm and with mighty acts of judgment," which is exactly what He did. This is vividly recorded in Exodus, chapters 7–11. It was through His power that, in chapter 7, Aaron's staff became a snake that swallowed up the staff of Pharaoh's sorcerers and magicians. In the same chapter, Aaron followed God's instructions to strike the water of the Nile with his staff, and all of Egypt's waterways became red with blood, killing the fish. This caused a great stink and made the water undrinkable for the people. In chapter 8, once again, following God's instructions, Aaron stretched out his staff over the water, and frogs came up and covered the land, going into the homes, ovens, and bedrooms, and even covered the people. Yet Pharaoh's heart was hardened, and he still refused to free God's people. It was also in chapter 8 that, when Aaron struck the dust of the ground with his staff, all the dust of Egypt became tiny, pesky gnats covering the people and their animals.

This was the point that Pharaoh's magicians said to Pharaoh in verse 19, "This is the finger of God," but his heart was hardened and he refused to listen. Later in chapter 8, God used Moses to warn Pharaoh of another impending plague if he continued to hold the Israelites captive. This time it would be swarms of flies, which, as the result of Pharaoh's refusal to heed the warning, covered the people and their houses and ruined the entire land. Finally, Pharaoh relented but then changed his mind and again refused to let the people go.

In chapter 9, Moses warned Pharaoh that the Lord would bring a plague on the Egyptians' horses, donkeys, camels, cattle, and sheep if he refused to let the people go. But again, Pharaoh refused, and all the livestock of the Egyptians died. In verse 10, the Egyptians themselves were plagued with painful, festering boils from the soot of a furnace, which became fine dust that the Lord instructed Moses to toss into the air. Continuing in chapter 9:14–18, God used Moses to confront Pharaoh with the following warning if he refused to let the Israelites go:

> This time I will send the full force of my plagues against you and against your officials and your people, so you may know there is no one like me in all the earth. For by now I could have stretched out my hand and struck you and your people with a plague that would have wiped you off the earth. But I have raised you up for this very purpose, that I might show you my power and that my name might be proclaimed in all the earth. You still set yourself against my people and will not let them go. Therefore, at this time tomorrow, I will send the worst hailstorm that has ever fallen on Egypt, from the day it was founded till now.

True to His word, the following day, the Lord instructed Moses to stretch out his hand with his staff toward the sky, and thunder crashed, hail rained down, and lightning flashed. Verse 24 tells us, "It was the worst storm in all the land of Egypt since it had become a nation," and verses 25–26 tell us, "Throughout Egypt, hail struck everything in the fields—both men and animals; it beat down everything growing in the fields and stripped every tree."

Following some bargaining with Moses and Aaron, Pharaoh agreed to let the people go, only to renege on it once Moses held up his part of the agreement. Chapter 10:1–3 records an important message that the Lord told Moses to give to Pharaoh; it speaks to us of the twenty-first century as well. "Then the Lord said to Moses, 'Go to Pharaoh, for I have hardened his heart and the hearts of his officials so that I may perform these miraculous signs of mine among them that you may tell your children and grandchildren how I dealt harshly with the Egyptians and how I performed my signs among them, and that you may know that I am the Lord.'" While Moses literally saw the plagues that God brought upon the land and people of Egypt, we can only read about them in His Word. But does this not speak to us as well? We, too, are to witness to our descendants of the immensity of His power as well as His love for us, His twenty-first-century people.

In his lack of humility and refusal to recognize this God of the Hebrews as Lord, Pharaoh continued to bring calamity upon his people. In chapter 10, as warned, the land was covered with swarms of locusts, entering the houses of the people and officials and eating anything that remained after the plague of hail, devastating the land. The ninth plague was one of total darkness; it was so dark that it could be felt, and no one was able to see another person or leave his or her home because of this blackness. This lasted for three days. Again, we see Pharaoh trying to bargain with Moses, and finally, in verse 28, Pharaoh says to Moses, "Get out of my sight! Make sure you do not appear before me again! The day you see my face, you will die." This brings us to the tenth and final plague. It is the one that finally persuaded Pharaoh to let the Israelites go. It is the plague on the firstborn and the worst of all the plagues, as it took the lives of all firstborn sons of Egypt, including that of Pharaoh's son on down to the slave girl's son and all firstborn cattle as well.

To make ready for that heartbreaking judgment, God gave Moses and Aaron detailed instructions for the community of Israelites to follow. What ensues in chapter 12 is their preparation for what is still celebrated by the Jewish community to this day. It is called the Passover. The Israelites were instructed to take a one-year-old sheep, one without defect, slaughter it, and put its blood on the sides and on the tops of the doorframes of their houses. We hear the somber instructions in verses 12–13 when the Lord speaks: "On that same night I will pass through Egypt and strike down every firstborn—both men and animals—and I will bring judgment on all the gods of Egypt. I am the Lord. The blood will be a sign for you on the houses where you are and when I see the blood, I will pass over you. No destructive plague will touch you when I strike Egypt." It was a night of loud wailing throughout Egypt because there was not an Egyptian house without someone dead as the Lord brought that last devastation on Egypt. It was what finally convinced Pharaoh to let God's people go.

While the consequences of this king's hard-heartedness caused great suffering and death to his people, it was this same God who made a distinction between the Egyptians and the Israelites, sparing His chosen ones the devastation and hardships created by those plagues. It was the God who loved them and called them to be His own that parted the waters of the Red Sea so they could cross on dry ground and escape Pharaoh's army. His love, compassion, and care for them continued as He led them through the desert in a pillar of cloud by day and a pillar of fire by night so they would know He was with them, guiding them and providing them with light so they could travel by day or by night. God had shown Himself in all these ways to be a caring, loving God who looked down upon these suffering people with compassion and who had fulfilled His promise to free them.

Now, free at last from Pharaoh's grip, we find them in the desert of Sinai, and the people are camped at the foot of the mountain. In Exodus 19:17, following previous instructions by God, we are told that, "Moses led the people out of the camp to meet with God. They stood at the foot of the mountain, which was covered with smoke because the Lord descended on it in fire; the whole mountain trembled violently and the sound of a trumpet grew louder and louder." God's people trembled with fear at the display of such mighty power, and as Moses descended the mountain, he told the people what God had said to him. He began by saying, "God spoke all these words: 'You shall have no other gods before me.'"

Through the plagues, we have discovered more than God's great power. We have seen His fierce love for His people and the lengths to which He went to keep His promise to free them. So, too, we of this twenty-first century are also the unworthy, but grateful recipients of His almighty power and great love. He has freed us also—not from the power of a Pharaoh, but from the power of the penalty due for our sin. It was through the sacrifice, death, and resurrection of His Son, Jesus Christ, that we have been freed. Indeed, He alone is God and is the only one worthy of all our worship and adoration.

Chapter 2

SINGLE-MINDEDNESS IS
YOUR ONLY OPTION

COMMANDMENT #2

"You shall not make for yourself an idol in the form of anything in heaven above or on the earth beneath or in the waters below. You shall not bow down to them or worship them; for I, the Lord your God, am a jealous God, punishing the children for the sin of the fathers to the third and fourth generation of those who hate me, but showing love to a thousand generations of those who love me and keep my commandments" (Exodus 20:4–6).

At first glance, it would seem that God is repeating Himself in this second command. However, a closer look tells us that He understands the length and breadth to which the imagination of humanity's minds will go to create those idols. In so doing, He rules out anything in heaven, on earth, or in the waters below. He could not make it any clearer. Nothing may be made into another god to take His place. He alone is God. Now, He is also saying, you may neither make them nor bestow honor on them by bowing down or worshipping them because, "I, the Lord your God, am a jealous God."

Strange, isn't it? In fact, by rescuing His people, He showed Himself to be a God of compassion, mercy, and love—hardly one who is jealous as we define jealousy. We think of it as a form of envy, which *Merriam-Webster's Dictionary* defines as having "a resentful desire for another's possessions," an attitude we consider sinful. We know that God is holy and does not sin, and as we look further, we find the word *jealousy* described as intolerance, disloyalty, or infidelity. Now, this is something we humans understand well. In our marriages, we jealously expect total fidelity to the vows made by both partners at their wedding. When these vows are broken, we experience a great sense of betrayal, which often results in the dissolution of the marriage bond and a great deal of emotional pain to all involved. Just as we desire to be the one and only to our mates, so too, God wants to be the one-and-only God in our lives, desiring an untainted relationship—one without us chasing after other false gods that would weaken our relationship with Him.

The question we need to ask ourselves is this: have we,

people of the twenty-first century, thoughtlessly made false gods of our possessions, money, and time? We are blessed to live at a time in history when we can take vacations, participate in sports, and be entertained by Hollywood films or by watching television, to name a few. Of course, this itself is not wrong. But what about when these things become our priorities and more important to us than attending a worship service, spending time in scripture, studying God's Word, and meeting with Him in prayer? Let's be honest; the more time we give to our earthly pleasures, the less time we have to give to our God in heaven.

An article called "Idols, Ancient and Modern," by Timothy J. Padgett, asks this question: "Are we idolators?" He goes on to say, "The same drives and impulses leading our more ignorant forebearers to bow down to wood and stone, push us to create our own little gods that are equally unable to save. We've got things like the TV show, *American Idol* and we very often speak of a sports media idol. But in these cases, we mean only a metaphorical idol. The attention and praise which we devote to some of these demigods make for an apt analogy for idolatry."

Mr. Padgett closes his article with this statement: "We often think of the dangers of idolatry in terms of disloyalty and infidelity, and this is true, but along with those failures come the inevitable effect that our little gods have on our lives. Whenever we limit God to our personal, cultural or idealized imaginations, He ceases to be the God of heaven and becomes instead merely the projections of our passions and desires." His article also mentions, "A god bound by the limitations of our preferences and confined by our judgments will only deify our already corrupted desires."

What, then, is our priority? The time we are given here on earth is a gift from God, and we need to seriously consider how we are spending it and what we are spending it on. Although we all need to consider those questions for ourselves, most important is this: is it hurting or enriching our relationships with our God?

Something else in this second command tends to give people pause for reflection, and that is when God speaks of punishing the children for the sins of the fathers to the third and fourth generation of those who hate Him. There are two facts we need to address. First, if God is a God of mercy and forgiveness, why would He do such a thing? We need to remember that He is also a holy and just God and therefore cannot allow sin to go unpunished. He may forgive, but just as we forgive our children for outright disobedience, they still suffer the consequences of it.

It is the consequences of sin that the parents pass on to their children, not the sin itself. Scripture does not tell us that we are held responsible for the sins of others but rather each person is answerable for his or her own. However, sinful patterns of behavior are often passed on to family members. When one is exposed daily to alcoholism, sexual abuse, or violence, a child can be negatively affected for his or her lifetime. Then there are those babies whose mothers were addicts while they were pregnant and who are now suffering the effects from the mothers' behaviors. A side note in an NIV Quest Study Bible helps to clarify this with the following explanation: "Sin has pervasive consequences and children are affected by alcoholic parents, for instance, and many victims of abuse become abusers themselves.

The Israelites, with their strong solidarity, knew that good and evil affected whole families, not just individuals. They recognized the ripple effect of sin throughout generations."

In the case of violence and child abuse, whether sexual or bodily harm in general, the article, "Long-Term Consequences of Child Abuse and Neglect," printed by www.childwelfare. gov, speaks to the perpetuation of abuse. "This cycle of maltreatment can be a result of children learning early on that physical abuse or neglect is an appropriate way to parent." We must be careful not to stand in judgement or misstate that these problems apply to all those who have experienced any one of these abuses in their early years. However, we must also have a keen awareness that the probability of these issues being passed on to future generations is highly possible and is often the experience of those targeted by abusers.

This commandment not only requires our total loyalty to the one who jealously guards His supremacy as the one and only God; it also closes the command with a note of hope and the promise of blessing to those who keep it. He promises His love to a thousand generations to come who will love Him and keep His commandments.

Chapter 3

WHAT'S IN A NAME?

COMMANDMENT #3

"You shall not misuse the name of the Lord your God, for the Lord will not hold him guiltless who misuses His name" (Exodus 20:7).

Expecting parents spend a good deal of time deciding on names for their new babies. In by-gone days, it was usually the name of either parent, depending on the child's gender, or the name of an esteemed relative. In this way, family names would be carried on for generations. Children were even named after a favored biblical person. In our twenty-first-century America, some parents hold to those traditions, while other choose the names of famous sport figures, from lists in baby books, while still others choose names we've never heard before.

In biblical times, most names had a particular meaning that, in some cases, indicated one's position, and in others, a personality or character trait. Names were even changed when one's status or circumstances changed. One of those instances, which Bible students are likely familiar with, is that of Abram and Sarai. In Genesis 17, God Himself changed their names to *Abraham* and *Sarah* upon confirming His covenant with Abram. He would become the father of many nations through his offspring, who had yet to be conceived. In John 1, Simon, a fisherman who became a disciple of Christ, was given the name *Cephas* by Jesus, which meant *Peter*, or the rock. It was after Simon Peter's admission to Christ that he believed Him to be the Christ, the Son of the living God, that Peter was given the spiritual authority by Jesus to preach the good news of the gospel. In the case of Abraham and Sarah and Simon Peter, new names were given that were specific to both circumstance and status. They also open our eyes to the presence and power of God in the lives of those He chooses to use in a special way for His good purposes.

How, then, does this relate to God's name? Having just considered that humans have created gods of all sorts for themselves throughout the ages, we need to ask just what it is that makes this God stand apart from all the others we've mentioned. Let's begin by saying that God always was, is, and always will be. He is without beginning or end. The first four words of the Bible makes that clear when it says, "In the beginning, God." He is alive and, since creating Adam and Eve, has always wanted a relationship with humankind. His name is above all names because of who He is: holy, perfect, and without sin. His name is also intentional in relation to His character, attributes, and very existence. All things belong to Him including all of creation. He is creator of all that was, is, and is to come.

In His dealings with us, He has shown mercy, compassion, and love to all humankind. Throughout the ages, He has extended His grace to all beings by supplying all things necessary for life itself, in the form of water, food, health, strength, daily protection, shelter, jobs, and our very breath. The list is endless. Then there are those emotional needs He has filled by providing us with mates, families, and friends who bring so much joy and pleasure into our lives.

These are just a few tangible blessings we enjoy daily as gifts from our Maker, yet we take for granted. Beyond these blessings are the wonders of God's attributes that we either aren't aware of, or don't give much thought to, yet they are innately present in the very essence of who He is. God is all-knowing, all-powerful, ever present, eternal, infinite, immutable, righteous, all-wise, and faithful, to name a few.

Though He is a God of mercy, love and grace, He is also a God who is just and therefore becomes angry when His name is misused.

Besides the fact that our casual use of the English language has become, for lack of a better word, sloppy, leaving much to be desired, it has also become a common practice to misuse God's holy name mindlessly and irreverently. However, that does not excuse us from the consequences of God's anger. We need to be reminded of what it means to swear, to curse, to damn, and to blaspheme.

The clearest and simplest explanations are found in *Merriam-Webster's Dictionary*. To swear is "to make a solemn promise, sometimes under oath." James 4:15 may sound archaic to us as contemporary people when he tells us that when making such a promise, we need to add, "if it is the Lord's will." His reason for this is that we don't know if we will be able to keep that promise since we don't know what tomorrow holds. Is that not true? An exception is in the case of a court of law where, as law-abiding citizens, we promise to tell the truth. To return to *Merriam-Webster's*, we're told that cursing is considered "an appeal for evil or injury to befall something or someone," while damning is "to condemn to eternal punishment" or "to pronounce adverse judgement on something or someone." Then there is blasphemy, which is "to speak of God irreverently."

In all these cases, we arrogantly put ourselves in a position of authority that belongs to God alone. In Old-Testament times, this was punishable by death. In Leviticus 24, when the son of an Israelite mother blasphemed God's name, verse 16 tells us that "anyone who blasphemes the name of the Lord should be put to death." While that may be the consequence of transgressing an Old Testament law, the fact remains that God is still God and is still holy. God has not changed. He remains to be the very same God of the twenty-first century that He was when He gave Moses these commandments.

We use our tongues loosely and need to be intentional in our thinking and speaking, lest we misuse God's name and stand before Him with a guilty verdict. Imagine how we would react if someone used our name in anger or in judgment against another person. It would also be wise to remember that Satan, the hater of God and tempter of humanity, loves it when we image-bearers of God use our tongues to speak the Lord's name in such harmful, hateful, and derogatory language against another one of His image-bearers.

James 3:9–10 gives us a graphic description of the inconsistency with which we use our tongues: "With the tongue we praise our Lord and Father, and with it we curse men, who have been made in God's likeness. Out of the same mouth comes praise and cursing. My brothers, this should not be." And Luke 6:45 echoes James's thought using different imagery: "The good man brings good things out of the good stored up in his heart, and the evil man brings evil things out of the evil stored up in his heart. For out of the overflow of his heart his mouth speaks."

God remains the same; He is still holy. Humanity remains the same; we are still born sinners. We still need the saving grace offered through God's Son, Jesus Christ, the one who kept all of these commandments perfectly in our stead. Regrettably, we continue to misuse our tongues but, thankfully, forgiveness is freely given when we ask for it. Ultimately, a wise person must guard his or her heart and, by God's grace, honor His Holy name.

Chapter 4

A GIFT FROM HEAVEN

COMMANDMENT #4

"Remember the Sabbath day by keeping it holy. Six days you shall do all your work but the seventh day is a Sabbath to the Lord your God. On it you shall not do any work, neither you, nor your son or daughter, nor your manservant or maidservant, nor your animals, nor the alien within your gates. For in six days the Lord made the heavens and the earth, the sea and all that is in them, but he rested on the seventh day. Therefore, the Lord blessed the Sabbath day and made it holy" (Exodus 20: 8–11).

There was a time when the Sabbath was considered a day to be set apart from the other six. Workers laid down their tools of the trade, offices were darkened, and stores were empty and quiet, their doors closed to the public. It wasn't even necessary to hang a "closed" sign in the window or on the door, as it was common knowledge to all that this was a day when our daily work came to a standstill. It was the Sabbath, a day of rest and worship. Of course, there were those, such as doctors and nurses, farmers who tended to their animals' needs, and other workers who provided necessities for and the care of others. In many households across America, preparation for the Sabbath began earlier in the week. All household work was taken care of, groceries were purchased, lawns were mowed, and cars were washed. On Saturday, clothes were pressed, shoes were polished, and all was made ready for the Sabbath.

The Sabbath was considered a special day to be set aside for going into God's house where worshippers, with a great sense of awe and respect for His holiness, presented themselves to worship their God. It was also a day of physical rest. Genesis 2:3 tells us that, "God blessed the Sabbath day and made it holy because on it He rested from all the work of creating that He had done." Being God, He certainly didn't need to rest, but He gave us the example of setting aside a day to rest and honor Him. He knew that after six days of long hours of busyness and hard work, our physical bodies needed time to be refreshed and reenergized. So, too, our emotional and spiritual needs had to be fed. Who would know this better than He, since it was He who created us? The Lord knew that when we pushed ourselves too hard and for too long, our bodies would rebel with resistance in the form of exhaustion or sickness; our minds would become too stressed to think clearly; and our spiritual lives would run dry.

What happens to our vehicles when we fail to maintain them with fresh oil, new air filters, and keep gas in the gas tank? They begin to run roughly, wear out, and eventually stop working. They fail to accomplish the purpose for which they were made. Our amazing bodies, which are so very intricately designed and created, also need to be given proper care. While we are physical beings, we are also spiritual beings that need to be refreshed from the daily forces of this world we live in. Worshipping our Creator in a special way on the Sabbath, hearing from His Word, approaching Him in prayer, and giving Him our thanks and praise, are all medicines for our spiritual health.

As far back as the eighteenth century, colonial New England introduced what was known as blue laws, which were eventually adopted by most states. Their main purpose was the observance of the Sabbath. Like many rules of the nineteenth and twentieth century, they included a great deal of differing opinions and human-made rules, much like the Pharisees of the New Testament did. In their effort to keep to the letter of the law, they lost the spirit of the law. However, by having all stores close on the same day, on the Sabbath or the Lord's Day, as it came to be called, both employers and employees were given a common day on which they could choose how they wanted to use it. As a result, one would find churches full and stores darkened and empty.

In the early seventies, retailers who saw no reason for Sunday closure began to open their doors on the Sabbath, and like-minded consumers gladly patronized them. Now, in the twenty-first century, nearly all retail stores are open on the Sabbath, as well as every day of the year, with the exception of Thanksgiving, Christmas Day, and Easter Sunday. Of course, there are always exceptions, depending on the owner's religious beliefs. There are also those who have chosen to limit their Sabbath hours for various reasons, some of which are based on economics or the necessity of the product they sell. For many people, shopping, eating out, attending entertainment of a sort, or even watching or participating in a sporting event is their choice and has become the way they choose to spend the Sabbath. This raises the question: we may be resting on the Sabbath, but are we keeping it holy, or has it simply become part of the leisure time we spend on ourselves?

All of this seems so far removed from the long-ago command of Exodus 20:8, "Remember the Sabbath day to keep it holy." *Holy* means to be set apart. It's as if God has made a weekly date to meet with us in a special way. It's also a weekly reminder that He is our God, and we are His people. Our knowledge of and relationship with Him grows as we listen to His Word spoken to us from the pulpit and as we worship with fellow believers.

Corporate worship gives one a sense of belonging, a belonging different than that of social gatherings. It is a oneness of mind and of purpose. We gain a special blessing from this time spent in spiritual worship; learning and growth is that we are then able to apply what we've learned to every aspect of our daily lives on the other six days of the week. In so doing, our honoring of God becomes part of our daily living and is not reserved only for the Sabbath.

When we are spiritually strong, so are our families, communities, and nation because we share a common and firm foundation for our existence as a people. And, by embracing this God-given gift of the Sabbath, we become better prepared to meet the demands life brings and become a positive force for good in the society in which we live.

Chapter 5

DOUBLE HONORS

COMMANDMENT #5

"Honor your father and mother, so that you may live long in the land the Lord your God is giving you" (Exodus 20:12).

At some point in our lives, this fifth commandment is the one that most of us will struggle with more than the others. Beginning with the "terrible twos," parents begin to wonder if *no* is the only word in their toddler's vocabulary. Then, there are those preteen years when children dare to question their parents' *no* to many of their requests. These years are followed by the rebellious teens, when Mom and Dad are often seen as the enemy who puts the brakes on all of their fun.

At last, the years of insight and realization arrive when the now-grown children marry and begin to raise their own children, and the moment of "Aha! Now I get it" arrives. In most families, parents who have graduated to the status of grandparents will be included in the lives of their grandchildren: babysitting, attending school events, and eventually, graduations and weddings. This all sounds so much like the normal progression in the lives of most families.

Sadly, for many great-grandparents or even great-great-grandparents, their statuses change from participants in family life to that of bystander. Now, possibly as residents in a nursing home or senior facility, some families feel the burden of caring for them lifted from their shoulders, and they go on with their lives. Nurses and chaplains who work in these homes see this as a common experience for many of their residents.

Since it is true that we may dishonor parents by disobeying, disrespecting, or by unintentional neglect, it seems necessary, at this point, to take the time to look at what the basis and intent of parenting is and why it was considered so important that God included it in the Ten Commandments.

In Genesis 1:27, we are told that God created humans in His image, male and female, and in verse 28, He tells them to be fruitful and increase in number. Leah Baugh wrote an article for *Core Christianity* in which she said, "God has given authority to various offices within the structure of his created order and one of those offices is the office of parent. The family was built into the fabric of creation from the beginning with Adam and Eve." They were given the mandate to multiply. Further in her article, Baugh continues, "The family structure not only provides for the population of the world but is also for the good of children and society in general. The fifth commandment relates directly to how God has ordained and ordered this world."

It is interesting to note that even among less civilized populations, children are obligated to honor their parents. Philosophers such as Plato and Aristotle both believed that parents were to be shown the highest respect. In the Talmud, the command to honor one's parents is compared to honoring God. We need to consider the tremendous responsibility given them. They must not only provide daily sustenance, shelter, protection, and schooling, but spiritual instruction as well.

Parents are to conduct themselves lovingly toward their children. In this way, the children may see God's love through their parents. They are not to use their authority by lording it over their children in an ungodly manner, but as God's Word tells us in Ephesians 6:4, "Fathers, do not provoke your children to anger, but bring them up in the discipline and instruction in the Lord." Unfortunately, it is true that there are parents who misuse this mandate to exercise their authority in abusive ways that harm their children both physically and emotionally. There are also those parents who demand that their children commit acts of behavior that are contrary to God's commandments.

God never promotes or rewards evil. In such cases, the child who finds him- or herself in such a difficult situation has the right to refuse obedience as Acts 5:29 instructs. After the apostles were given power to heal and preach the good news of Christ and the resurrection of the dead in Him, the jealous Sadducees, who did not believe in the resurrection of the dead, had them thrown in jail. They were later brought before the high priest and Sanhedrin, who reminded them that they were given strict orders not to teach in the name of Jesus. Their reply was, "We must obey God rather than men!" Obviously, their situation was different than that of an abused or misused child, but the principle is the same: when orders are given that are contrary to God's law or ways, obeying Him comes first.

Often, the Bible provides instructions for general situations and, at other times, for specific situations. In specific instances, however, we must be truly sure we are using our refusal to obey legitimately. The most well-known failure to show love and respect, followed by repentance and forgiveness, is that of the prodigal son in Luke 15. Here was a young man who decided he didn't want to wait until his wealthy father died to receive his inheritance, so he arrogantly asked his father to give it to him then. Essentially, it was as if the son was telling his father he wished he was dead so he could have his inheritance now. And, surprisingly, his father complied.

After wasting his money in wild living and finding himself starving and in dire straits, the son comes to his senses, sees the foolishness of his ways, and returns home, where he finds his father running to meet him with a kiss and open arms. He confesses his foolishness to his father, who then has a feast prepared in celebration of his son's return. In verse 24, we hear the happy father say, "For this son of mine was dead and is alive again, he was lost and is found." What love! What a beautiful picture of our heavenly Father waiting on us to make that spirit-led choice to come to our senses and to seek out His forgiveness and fatherly compassion, to feel His open arms welcoming us as we, His sons and daughters, confess our sins and disobedience against Him. Our heavenly Father is the perfect mentor for everyone.

This commandment is the first one with a promise in relation to our particular response to it. It is more than a matter of obeying our parents. It's also a matter of honoring them, which includes respect and admiration. That comes from within one's heart. On the other hand, obedience can be given with a resentful and hostile attitude. We arrive at the point of honoring them when we take into consideration all that our parents have done for us, including sacrifices they have made on our behalf. That may be truer as we come into adulthood and recognize it as we begin to parent our own children. We can then begin to realize the value of them having been God's representative in our lives. We may no longer be expected to obey our parents, but God expects us to honor them always. This is very important to God, when in Exodus 20:12, He adds this to the command to honor your father and mother: "So that you may live long in the land the Lord your God is giving you." It is true that this promise was given to the Israelites, who He was bringing into the land of Canaan, which He had promised them, but they were also given to all humankind, including us, by way of His word.

We have seen the devastation and heartbreak brought onto families by young people who disobeyed and dishonored their parents by way of drug and alcohol use, drunk driving, wild parties, and sexual misconduct to name just a few. Sadly, such behaviors often result in the premature loss of young lives. This is not meant to suggest that all young people who honor and obey their parents are guaranteed smooth sailing, but once again, the general principle that respectful responses to limitations set by parents have God's blessing.

There is yet another equation to this honoring of parents. With divorce being so prevalent in our contemporary society, children are often torn, as they are made to feel they must choose one parent over the other, particularly in cases where there is much anger and bitterness between their parents. They struggle with a variety of questions, a big one for them being, who do I obey—Mom or Dad? Also, in the case of remarriage, whether it follows divorce or the death of one's partner, the new spouse is often treated with resentment, hurtful words, and cold shoulders—in essence, treated disrespectfully. Unfortunately, this type of behavior has a ripple effect that hurts the entire family and their relationships.

What does God expect of us in these situations? His makes it clear in His Word that we are to show respect and honor regardless of our age; whether we are a child or an adult, we are never to speak or act disrespectfully to anyone. Philippians 2:1–4 gives us instructions for all situations into which life brings us: "If you have any encouragement with being united with Christ, if any comfort from His love, if any fellowship with the Spirit, if any tenderness and compassion, then make my joy complete by being like-minded, having the same love, being one in spirit and in purpose. Do nothing out of selfish ambition or vain conceit, but in humility consider others better than yourselves. Each of you should look not only to your own interests, but also to the interests of others." While Paul was writing to the believers in Philippi, he was writing to us as well. And in Romans 12:9, he exhorts us to "honor one another above yourselves."

Honoring parents is a prerequisite to the teaching of the law from one generation to the next. How can we teach this fifth commandment to our children if we ourselves dishonor our parents, stepparents, or grandparents? This is a question that needs to be given serious, honest consideration. Scripture makes it clear in Ephesians 6:1, "Children, obey your parents in the Lord, for this is right." Proverbs 1:8 also gives us wise instruction: "Hear, my son, your father's instruction and forsake not your mother's training." It was God who gave parents authority over their children. We must remember that when God gave these commands, it was to both parents and their children, who were standing at the foot of the mountain. They were to be passed on from generation to generation. Most importantly, it is this God of the Israelites and of the twenty-first century who makes it clear that by honoring our parents, we honor Him.

We may conscientiously wonder if we are honoring our parents as we should. We all live by a common code of proper conduct with which we are familiar and that tells us when we have broken it. Some call it our conscience. Believers call it the Holy Spirit, who gives our minds disquiet and unease, with a sense of guilt or shame. Conversely, we may also wonder how we can display our love, esteem, and honor for our aging parents in ways other than seeing to their daily well-being. We are used to recognizing them in their roles as our parents, but we often fail to recognize them as individuals, or as people. They have had a lifetime of experiences and relationships. They have had good times and difficult times, disappointments, and heartaches. At one time, they had jobs, hopes, and dreams for their futures that may or may not have become reality. They have so much knowledge and wisdom to offer if only we would spend time with them and ask them about themselves. We need to look at them with our hearts.

It is a good thing to be reminded that Christ set the supreme example for us when He was on the cross. He spoke to his mother and to His disciple, John, as recorded in John 19:26: "When Jesus saw His mother there," near the cross on which he hung, and the disciple whom He loved standing nearby, He said to His mother, 'Dear woman, here is your son' and to the disciple, 'here is your mother.' From that time on, this disciple took her into his home." Even at the point of death, Jesus made sure His mother would be cared for. Here was a son who truly honored His mother.

Chapter 6
LIFE IS PRECIOUS

COMMANDMENT #6

"You shall not murder" (Exodus 20:13).

Looking at this sixth commandment prompts one to wonder why God included this particular one with the other nine. After all, what ordinary, law-abiding citizen would ever consider murdering another human being? But then, remember Cain? In Genesis 4, we read about the first murder committed by one brother against another. Cain, who was most likely jealous, became angry that God had accepted his younger brother, Abel's, offering and refused his own. As a result, his heart began to harbor dark, evil thoughts of murder. Cain, though warned by God that his sound reasoning was being overcome by the hatred in his heart, invited Abel to go out to the fields together, and there he attacked and murdered him. Afterward, when God confronted him and asked where Abel was, Cain arrogantly answered with that often-quoted reply, "Am I my brother's keeper?"

Taking another's life is unthinkable to us, yet we hear of it and even watch it happening daily on our television screens. What is it that causes such life-shattering acts of evil to be taken against another? Sadly, we humans find ourselves prone to envy and spite and greed. Two other elements often involved in the case of murder are extreme anger and hate, such as we've seen in Cain's heart. Synonyms that better express the degree of hate are those of loathing and despising someone. Another obvious contribution is that of hostility or enmity that, according to *Merriam-Webster's Dictionary*, is "deep-rooted hatred, usually in a relationship where feelings of hatred are mutual."

Consideration of this command can pull us in many directions and poses several questions. For example, what are the differences between murdering or killing someone and euthanasia? What determines the degree of punishment involved? What about sanctuary cities? First, there is a definite distinction between the act of murder and that of killing. According to our United State Courts, first-degree murder is generally intentional and premeditated and is without legal justification. Its intent is to kill. Killing, which is still taking another's life, is given much more leeway. The general term is *homicide*, and it is used broadly. According to an explanation by MurphysLawOffice.org, "Homicide may or may not be legal such as in war or when defending oneself when threatened by an intruder. Then there is voluntary and involuntary manslaughter which usually involves acts of provocation or acts of negligence or recklessness leading to a person's death."

Answering these questions about laws and, in some cases, where it becomes political, belongs to those more qualified and capable of answering them. What we need to grasp and understand is the answer to this question: what is the underlying principle of the command not to murder? Genesis 1:26–27 tells us that at the time of creation, God said, "Let us make man in our image, in our likeness, and let them rule over the fish of the sea and the birds of the air, over the livestock, over all the earth, and over all the creatures that move along the ground. So God created man in His own image, in the image of God He created him; male and female He created them." And in Genesis 5:1, God's Word says, "When God created man, He made them in the likeness of God. He created them male and female and blessed them. And when they were created, He called them man." In these texts, God has given humanity the mandate to rule His creatures and creation. Humans are the crowning glory of His creation, blessed with intelligence, wisdom, and the ability to reason and not live by instinct alone as with the animal kingdom. We can communicate with speech and make plans. Though we are made in God's image, we do not bear a physical image of our creator since He is spirit (John 4:24). However, it doesn't change the fact that, as His image-bearers, we are able to reflect many of His attributes, such as love, compassion, mercy, holiness, and forgiveness.

A Focus on the Family article, "What It Means to Be Made in the Image of God," takes the following position, as do many Christians:

> Knowing that we are made in God's image affects not only our understanding of our Creator and our relationship in him. It also sets the stage for understanding and defending the sanctity of human life. Every single human being, no matter how much the image of God is marred by sin, or illness, or weakness, or age, or any other disability, still has the status of being in God's image and therefore must be treated with the dignity and respect that is due as God's image-bearer. This has profound implications for our conduct toward others. It means that people of every race deserve equal dignity and rights. It means that elderly people ... and children yet unborn deserve full protection and honor as human beings.

This takes us full circle back to "you shall not murder." Our attitude is most likely the one we began this chapter with: who would even consider murdering another human being? "Not I," we smugly answer. But the heart of this command is found in Matthew 5:21–22. Jesus said, "You have heard that it was said to the people long ago, 'Do not murder, and anyone who murders will be subject to judgment.' But I tell you that anyone who is angry with his brother will be subject to judgment." The verses that follow this offer wisdom on how to deal with such feelings and proposes conduct that helps us become reconciled to our adversary. You'll note that in verse 25 of the same chapter, Jesus counsels us to settle the matter quickly.

The point here is that the longer we allow feelings of anger to linger, the more room we are giving them to grow into seeds of hate and hateful actions, just as they did with Cain. Matthew 5:38–42 gives us instructions against using acts of personal revenge against evil people, and in a side note, the NIV Quest Study Bible explains it this way: "Jesus is setting forth the way to break the vicious cycle of retaliation. God's people are to work for justice but not take personal revenge. Elsewhere, the Bible makes it clear that Christians are to resist the devil (James 4:7) and the forces of evil that are in society (Ephesians 6:13)." Leviticus 19:18 states this clearly when the Lord says, "Do not seek revenge or bear a grudge against one of your people, but love your neighbor as yourself."

God alone is the giver of life, and He alone has the right to take a life. We need to remember that being created in God's image also gives us the ability to extend grace and forgiveness as His Spirit enables us, when we intend, as God told Cain, "To do what is right."

There is another way to look at this command. Telling us not to murder implies that our intent should be on conducting ourselves in a positive manner. Matthew 15:13 is often quoted and speaks to this matter: "Greater love has no one than this, that he lay down his life for his friends." Being made in God's image means more than refusing to take another person's life. It also implies the opposite: we should be willing to give our lives for our fellow humans. Many of our soldiers, police officers, and firefighters have done exactly that on our behalf.

There are also selfless, giving people everywhere who work endlessly for the sake of the hungry, the homeless, and the down-trodden. There are countless organizations that exist to help those whose lives have been turned upside down by natural disasters. Then there are those who spend their lives, some even giving their lives, spreading the word of God's love to thousands so that they may have eternal life. While not everyone has special abilities or training to serve in such life-saving capacities, the important element here is that being an image-bearer of God means that He has gifted every one of us in one way or another. While we may not be in public service, we can all honor and respect those who are, pray for them, and encourage them in their work. We have all been given talents and abilities that we can intentionally use to bless others. As we carry on with everyday living and activities in our jobs, communities, homes, and churches, we can display the answer to Cain's question, "Am I my brother's keeper?" by our conduct and attitude toward others.

What does all of this have to do with not committing murder? It's much more than just obeying God's command. It's breathing fresh life into it by our acts of mercy, compassion, concern, and love for others. Consider these words spoken to Cain by God himself; they are found in Genesis 4:6–7: "Why are you angry? Why is your face downcast? If you do what is right, will you not be accepted? But if you do not do what is right, sin is crouching at your door; it desires to have you, but you must master it."

Chapter 7

WHAT'S IN YOUR HEART?

COMMANDMENT #7

"You shall not commit adultery" (Exodus 20:7).

Most of us have shared the happiness and excitement that emanates from a couple who are standing face to face, looking into each other's emotion-filled eyes as they recite their vows to "love and cherish as long as they both shall live." This solemn ceremony is usually followed by a gathering of family and friends in a joyous celebration, with everyone wishing them well and many years of happiness. Although there are many considerations in setting up a new home, how many of us, being caught up in the emotions of romantic love, have stopped to consider what marriage is really about? How many of us have thought about what our expectations of marriage are; what expectations do we have of our new spouses and what might our spouses' expectations be of ourselves?

If these important elements of marriage are well thought out, discussed, and agreed upon before the big day, the future can be very promising for the newlyweds. But what if they have not previously given serious thought to these issues? What happens when the celebration and partying is all over, and we're faced with the demands and reality of bills that our budget didn't cover, our spouses having a bad day at work, or possibly even losing their jobs? Things are just not working out as they had hoped. She finds out her new husband leaves his clothes strewn all over the house for her to pick up, and he discovers that his wife isn't the gourmet chef he was hoping for. Perhaps it's something as simple as his needing to be in control of the television remote or her wondering why she must keep her figure while he loses his. These are things that can add up and create a pile of complaints and frustrations in marriages that no one thought about and that, with good communication and patience, can be overcome. We really need a reality check on this business called marriage. What is it all about anyway, and whose idea was it?

To answer those questions, we need to begin at the beginning. In Genesis 4:18, the Lord God said, "It is not good for the man to be alone. I will make a helper suitable for him." Verse 21 continues that thought:

> So the Lord God caused the man to fall into a deep sleep; and while he was sleeping, He took one of the man's ribs and closed up the place with flesh. Then the Lord God made a woman from the rib He had taken out of man, and He brought her to the man. The man said, "This is now bone of my bones and flesh of my flesh; she shall be called woman because she was taken out of man." For this reason, a man will leave his father and mother and be united to his wife, and they will become one flesh.

This is born out once again in the New Testament, when some of the Pharisees came to Jesus to test Him by asking whether it was lawful for a man to divorce his wife for any and every reason. It is important to understand that in Jesus's day, women had little legal protection and could be divorced simply because they displeased their husbands. Jesus answers them with the following question and answer in Matthew 19:4–6: "Haven't you read that at the beginning, the Creator made them male and female and said, 'For this reason a man shall leave his father and mother and be united to his wife and the two shall become one flesh. So they are no longer two but one. Therefore, what God has joined together, let not man separate.'" Furthermore, when the Pharisees continued to press Jesus, asking why Moses permitted a man to divorce his wife and send her away, Jesus replied in verse 8, "Moses permitted you to divorce your wives because your hearts were hard, but it was not that way from the beginning." This doesn't leave any room for debate that it was our Creator, God, who instituted the state of marriage and intended it to last until the death of one of the spouses.

So, what is it that happens to those couples when the honeymoon phase is over and they find themselves in a constant state of dissatisfaction with their spouses—and married life as a whole? What happened to the happiness and excitement of that wedding day that they so eagerly looked forward to and so joyously celebrated? It may happen quickly, or it may take years to come to the point of considering divorce, but sadly, it has become a common occurrence in our society and throughout the world.

Although this book is not about solving marriage problems, we would do well to look at those variables that contribute to broken homes. We could say that life happens, but life affects every marriage, and the vast majority of them survive. The question remains then, what makes the difference? Every expert has his or her own opinion and statistics, but there is some agreement about certain elements and behaviors that are primary in causing one to file for divorce. Lack of money, lack of communication, and lack of equality head the list, but there are other behaviors that are just as guilty, if not more so, of causing misery and unhappiness in a marriage. Abuse, both verbal and physical, addiction to alcohol, drugs, gambling, and pornography are all possible and obvious destroyers of a marriage and of family relationships. Then there is the one that becomes a devastating betrayer of that covenant made between the couple and before God Himself, none other than the subject of this seventh commandment: adultery.

According to *Merriam-Webster's Dictionary*, adultery is "voluntary sexual intercourse between a married person and a partner other than the lawful spouse." An article in BibleTools.org explains it this way: "The seventh commandment, forbidding adultery, unfaithfulness by either spouse stands against anyone who would defile the sanctity of the marriage covenant through sexual sins. Adultery is probably the most dishonest act against the binding contract of the marriage relationship; it is the betrayal of a most sacred trust."

It is also interesting to learn that the term *adulteration* is described as something that pollutes. In the case of marriage, it pollutes it with secrecy, lies, anger, fear, distrust, hurt, and betrayal. It reaches beyond the couple themselves; it breaks up the structure of the family, and furthermore, the structure of society as a whole. There are many forms used by clergy for the marriage ceremony. One from the 1987 edition of the Psalter hymnal, published by CRC Publications, describes the purpose of marriage in the following words: "In putting His blessing on a marriage, God intended that it would provide a context within which husband and wife can help and comfort each other and find companionship; a setting within which we may give loving and tender expression to the desires God gave us; a secure environment within which children may be born and taught to know and serve the Lord; and a structure that enriches society and contributes to its orderly function. When these purposes are prayerfully pursued in union with Christ, the kingdom of God is advanced and the blessedness of husband and wife assured."

Unfortunately, we live in a world broken by sin. Daily, we have temptation set before us on websites, in magazines, books, fashion, movies, television, advertising, and social media, to name a few. It would be well to state at this point that Jesus speaks to these means of temptation when He says, in Matthew 5:27–28, "You have heard that it was said, 'Do not commit adultery. But I tell you that anyone who looks at a woman lustfully has already committed adultery with her in his heart.'" After reading that warning, we would do well to heed the wise instruction of Proverbs 4:23. "Above all else, guard your heart, for it is the wellspring of life." And it is in the heart where this sin begins.

When we witness our society's liberal attitude on sex, when it is daily paraded in front of our eyes by the different forms of media, and when the ten commandments are viewed as outdated, unnecessary, and nothing more than a moral code since there are no longer any absolutes, our marriages and family structures become threatened. It has been said that a country is only as strong as it's families, yet we are witnessing a slow-but-sure weakening of a once-positive stronghold of our country.

The causes of the breakdown of marriage, including adultery, are many and are the subject of a host of books. While that has been discussed in small measure in this book, there is an important element that is missing in many unhappy marriages and that is crucial and of particular impact in creating and solidifying a good marriage. We need to face the truth: we are all sinners.

We all have things about ourselves that can bring out the ugliness that lies deep within each one of us. Yet, there are a large percentage of marriages that have a shared and strong foundation—their faith in God. This is more than a nominal practice of faith. These are couples who faithfully attend religious services of their choice, who practice the study of God's Word, who both individually and as a couple pray together, and who teach their children these practices and the importance they will bear on their lives as a whole. Homes that are built upon God's Word and commands for our well-being become the foundation of a Christian society.

In Mark 3:24–25, Jesus tells us this: "If a kingdom is divided against itself, that kingdom will not stand. If a house is divided against itself, that house cannot stand." Although Jesus didn't speak these words within the context of the seventh commandment, the underlying principle is the same; as a married couple, we are no longer two but one. How can a body then be divided against itself? In the context of this command, it is by betrayal of one half of that body to the covenant made to the other half. A happy home needs harmony, a pulling together for all members, whether that be a couple and their children or just a couple. That includes faithfulness and total commitment to their spouses and the well-being of their marriages.

So, the question remains—does having a solid foundation of abiding and practicing faith in God guarantee us a trouble-free marriage? Does it ban all sexual temptations as well as other problems? The answer is no. As already stated, we are all sinners, and thankfully, forgiven sinners. However, when God is at the center of our homes, when our hearts are centered on the way He wants us to live, we are more fully equipped to act responsibly and deal with all thoughts and behaviors that are contrary to His commands. Our homes are then enabled to become more stable because they are built on the solid foundation of God's Word.

Chapter 8

A LABOR OF LOVE

COMMANDMENT #8

"You shall not steal" (Exodus 20:15).

"Anyone who has been stealing must steal no longer, but must work, doing something useful with their own hands, that they may have something to share with those in need" (Ephesians 4:28). It is evident from this text in the New Testament that stealing is nothing new to humanity. Traveling long distances on those lonely country roads was dangerous for travelers, as robbers often lay in wait to take their belongings and even harm them physically. In the Old Testament, we saw a different form of stealing when Jacob stole his brother Esau's birthright. The book of Ecclesiastes so wisely tells us in chapter 1, in the closing of verse 9, that, "There is nothing new under the sun." This is a problem that people of the twenty-first century are dealing with as well.

We all know what it means to steal. The second edition of *The Believer's Bible Commentary*, written by William MacDonald and published by Thomas Nelson, talks about stealing this way: "It may take many forms—all the way from grand larceny to nonpayment of debts, to plagiarism, to the use of false measurements and to falsify expense accounts. The law of Moses forbade theft (Exodus 20:15). It is what follows that makes the passage distinctly Christian. Not only should we refrain from stealing; we should actually labor in an honorable occupation in order to be able to share with others who are less fortunate."

When we consider the issue of stealing, we generally think in terms of threatening, evil, gun-toting, masked men breaking into someone's house and helping themselves to their valuables or perhaps approaching tellers at gunpoint at the local bank. These may be the robberies that make the six o'clock news, but there are many facets of stealing that we fail to consider or perhaps don't even think of in those terms.

We humans like to rationalize our behaviors in terms of an act being bad or not so bad. We also tend to compare our conduct to other people's, thinking that ours isn't as bad as theirs. Yet, God doesn't differentiate between small and large theft. He does not split hairs like we so often do to justify our behaviors. In His eyes, stealing is stealing.

An article in BibleTools.org, the "Forerunner Commentary," has this to say about the eighth commandment: "This commandment is interwoven with the other commandments. Breaking it usually begins with covetousness. Such greed can lead to physical or mental violence and murder. It often involves fraud, deceit, trickery and lying. This commandment is God's affirmation that every human being has the right to private property and that others have no right granted by God to take that property for themselves without lawful permission."

A form of stealing we may glibly talk about yet fail to understand its impact on the average consumer is one that involves the retail world. A National Retail Security Survey conducted annually by the National Retail Federation trade group found that "the most missing inventory, 36.5 percent, was attributed to shoplifting by outside customers followed by employee theft of 30 percent, vendor fraud accounted for 5.4 percent, and 21.3 percent were due to administrative errors." The survey, which included eighty-three retailers, found that "the average cost per shoplifting incident was $798.41. The average cost per employee theft incident was $1,922.80. That was attributed in part to a lack of punitive action against shoplifters and employees. This theft cost the United States retail industry nearly fifty billion dollars in the year 2018. It cost each family in the United States a minimum of three to four hundred dollars per year to subsidize what shoplifters steal." Then there is identity theft, which touches hundreds of thousands of lives each year. It costs the public not only hundreds and more to retrieve their good credit ratings but also their reputations as responsible borrowers. We need to face the fact that there are all forms of stealing being carried out daily. And our excuses for them are as varied as the acts themselves.

The right to private and personal property is important to us as a society. Although any act of stealing is frowned on and is considered punishable by God, there is one other act of stealing that God speaks of in His Word. In the last book of the Old Testament, Malachi 3:8, God tells the descendants of Jacob that they were robbing Him by failing to bring the full measure of their tithe to Him. This goes back to the Mosaic Law in Leviticus 27:30: "A tithe of everything from the land, whether grain from the soil or fruit from the trees, belongs to the Lord; it is holy to the Lord." This referred to a tenth of their crops and was a law between the Israelites and God.

Although it is not viewed as something that applies to New-Testament Christians, we are expected to give, not out of duty, but out of gratitude for all the blessings God has bestowed on us. If we are withholding our offerings because our priorities are misplaced, then we need to ask ourselves if we are robbing God. It's a matter of the heart. It's true that, for many, resources are limited, but when our hearts are right with God, we will give the best that we are able. These gifts are given to help support those who minister to us. They are also used to help the needy and to support and advance the kingdom of God, whether it be Christian institutions, other charitable institutions, or to support those missionaries who so generously give of themselves to bring the good news of Jesus Christ to those who have not yet heard of Him and the salvation He so freely offers to all.

In light of all that's been said, it has become obvious that we humans have a real problem with obeying this eighth commandment. We need to look beyond ourselves and glean an awareness that there is a positive aspect to this command that reflects our responsibility toward others, their possessions, and their needs. We are to look after our neighbor's welfare as well as our own. The motivating principle of this command is more than simply not stealing. In Acts 20:35, in Paul's farewell to the Ephesian elders, he reminds them of the words of Jesus Himself, who said, "It is more blessed to give than to receive."

Chapter 9

NOTHING BUT THE TRUTH

COMMANDMENT # 9

"You shall not give false testimony against your neighbor" (Exodus 20:16).

This ninth commandment brings to mind Genesis 3:4, where the father of lies and hater of all that is godly introduced the very first lie into this world. Here it is that he lied to Eve. He contradicted God's warning to her that she should not eat of the tree of the knowledge of good and evil, as she and Adam would die. Satan told her this was not true, and she believed him. The truth was that, in time, they would die a physical death but also, at the moment of their disobedience to God, they died spiritually. Sadly, Eve believed Satan's lie. We stand just as guilty as Adam and Eve when we believe a lie one tells us about another, causing that person a great deal of grief.

Although the Lord gave this ninth commandment to all of the Israelites, it was directed, in particular, to those who might someday find themselves as a witness in a court of law. It was of utmost importance that they be truthful, as the lives of the accused hung heavily upon their testimonies. The same command applies to us. Whether we are in a court of law or speaking in a conversational manner to others, we need to be sure to guard our tongues. Our tainted speech may result in the loss of one's reputation, livelihood, self-esteem, or even one's freedom or loss of life. Most everyone knows that giving false testimony is a malicious false statement that is made to injure and cause harm to someone. Is that not what happened to Jesus? His was one of the most well-known trials of all times that ended in the greatest miscarriage of justice in the history of humanity. He was falsely accused by religious leaders, who brought additional false witnesses to testify against Him. If there was ever anyone who was denied a fair trial, it was Jesus. In fact, there was not even a pretense of a fair trial; they just wanted to be rid of Him, and so they called for His death.

Another element of false testimony is slander. According to *Merriam-Webster's Dictionary*, this includes "outright lying, deception, back-biting, or bearing tales." It even includes relating a report about someone without checking the truth of it. Leviticus 19:16 admonishes both the Israelites and us with these words: "Do not go about spreading slander among your people." And Exodus 23:1, when speaking of laws and justice, warns us, "Do not spread false reports about someone; do not help a wicked man by being a malicious witness."

Two other practices that are guilty of causing damage to others are silence and innuendoes. How often have we heard something malicious being reported about someone and, though we know it to be untrue, have kept silent? Does that not make us just as guilty as the person spreading the lies? The second practice, which is sneakier, is the innuendo. This is a sly ruse that makes an indirect or subtle derogatory implication. Another word to describe it is *insinuation*. It's an underhanded, slanderous deception that can damage one's reputation and character by lessening other's esteem of a person. It's what we call character assassination.

The things we say matter; our words carry weight. We have already mentioned many ways we devise to bring harm and ruin to others, but one we have not yet touched on is gossip. This is nothing less than "rumor, often of a personal or intimate and sensational nature," according to *Merriam-Webster's Dictionary*. An article from Bible.org, "The Sanctity of Truth," written by Robert L. Deffinbaugh, offers this to say about gossip: "If we have learned anything about communication over the centuries it is that even when we try to convey a given truth, it often comes out somewhat distorted. The well-known game of 'gossip' is but another evidence of the same phenomenon. When we add to this the act of the fall of humanity and the sinful inclination of our hearts, it is apparent that our speech will be corrupted and distorted."

There are numerous devices we use to hurt one another, some of them intentional and some of them out of thoughtlessness and a quick, sharp tongue. Speech is a gift from God, and, in most instances, it reveals what is in our hearts. Unless we are deeply rooted in God's Word, which commands us to be truthful, we could find ourselves numbered among those guilty of hurting the lives of others with our tongues. This raises the question, what causes us to be so hurtful to our human brothers and sisters as well as to our brothers and sisters in Christ?

The heart of this sinful behavior has already been touched upon, which is our own sinful nature. In our desire to elevate oneself in the eyes of others, we often do so by tearing down another, an unsuspecting victim. The reasons are numerous: envy, jealousy, hatred, vindictiveness, and the desire to hurt another person. There are times our hurtful and damaging words are intentional but are often spoken under the guise of innocence. Other practices, such as exaggerations and half-truths, are like a snake in the grass, sly and slithering their way into a conversation to attack an unsuspecting victim with poisonous words. Do we consider that when we spout off words about another person, they are usually taken seriously and as truth, as was just pointed out in Mr. Deffinbaugh's article?

The underlying principle of this command is justice and righteousness. Simply put, it means to meet the standards of what is right and just. Proverbs spells this out for us in chapter 4:23–24: "Above all else, guard your heart, for it is the wellspring of life. Put away perversity from your mouth; keep corrupt talk from your lips."

Before closing this chapter, we need to consider one other very—probably most—important matter of false testimony. The law was God's definition of righteousness, and when we injure another party through false testimony, we need to be aware that we are not only hurting him or her, but we are hurting ourselves as well. How? It hurts our relationship with God. We are all His image-bearers, and when we intentionally set out to hurt another of His image-bearers, He becomes very displeased with us.

God expects more from us; He expects obedience to His command to "love one another" and to "love our neighbors as ourselves." To state this in a positive way, we find direction from Zechariah (one of God's prophets) in Zechariah 8:16–17. He was told by God to bring this word to His people, which included those of us living in the twenty-first century as well as the Old-Testament Israelites. "These are the things you are to do. 'Speak the truth to each other, and render true and sound judgments in your courts; do not plot evil against your neighbor, and do not love to swear falsely. I hate all this, declares the Lord.'"

Chapter 10

CONTENTMENT

COMMANDMENT #10

"You shall not covet your neighbor's house. You shall not covet your neighbor's wife, or his manservant or maidservant, his ox or donkey, or anything that belongs to your neighbor" (Exodus 20:17).

H aving just finished looking at the last five commandments, we have seen that the way we conduct ourselves toward our neighbors is important to our relationship with both them and with our God. Although these ten commands are related by virtue of what's in our hearts, how we behave, and what our attitudes are toward our fellow humans and toward God, this tenth commandment is different. It speaks to a behavior that can be hidden because it stems from our minds. It is most often unspoken, left to fester in our minds and hearts. Although it is able to manifest itself in ungodly behavior, it begins with what we think as opposed to what we openly do. This is not to say that our hearts don't play a part in it, but we dare say it begins in our mind's eye.

Coveting is to feel an envious desire for something that belongs to another. It's one of those insidious itches that can seduce and entrap us. It grows from a bit of envy or jealousy into outright obsessive desire. While it is one of many of those old, soiled rags of our sinful natures, that doesn't mean we are helpless against controlling such desires; God is there to help us overcome our coveting if we ask for His help. Unfortunately, too often we allow our desires to breed many of these longings, enabling them to produce sinful behaviors such as lying, adultery, and, in some cases, even criminal acts, such as stealing and murder. King David is a prime example of what can happen when one flirts with coveting. In 2 Samuel 11, it describes what happened when he lusted and coveted after Bathsheba, the wife of his warrior Uriah; David's coveting led to adultery and Bathsheba's consequential pregnancy. To worsen matters, his solution was a murderous one. He had Uriah put in the front line of attack so he would be killed, and David could later claim Bathsheba as his wife and the child as his son. James 1:14 speaks of the progression of coveting this way, "But each one is tempted when, by his own evil desire, he is dragged away and enticed. Then, after desire has conceived, it gives birth to sin, and sin, when it is full-grown, gives birth to death." Such desires may begin in our minds but become a matter of the desires of our heart, a heart of discontent.

At one time or another, most of us look at possessions of our neighbors and think about how nice it would be to have something they have. We think of how it would make our lives easier or more comfortable. Perhaps we think of how nice it would be to have their status or popularity or even a bit of their wealth, which would ease our concerns over meeting our financial obligations. Although these are passing thoughts for most of us, some become obsessed with these thoughts to the point of coveting. While this command includes some possessions, such as house servants, which the average family does not have—neither are most of us owners of working animals—we do have other possessions. Notice that God did not leave this command wide open for us to guess what He was referring to. He finishes this command by pointedly stating we should not covet "anything that belongs to your neighbor."

We live in a society that is driven, in a large part, by competition. We are constantly bombarded with creative advertising whose goal is to convince us that we must have their products. This power of suggestion, often given to us by Facebook, Instagram, and Pinterest, to name a few, can easily take hold of our minds. This doesn't necessarily mean that advertising leads to coveting, but does it not often make us discontent with what we do have? If we truly desire to obey this tenth commandment, we need to guard our minds and be intentional about learning to be content with what God has given us. Luke reminds us of what Jesus said in His parable about the rich fool: "Watch out! Be on your guard against all kinds of greed; a man's life does not consist of the abundance of his possessions" (Luke 12:15). Jesus was not saying that it is wrong to be rich, but that if our hope is in what we possess and not in God, we are fools because when our lives end, we will then have nothing and no one, no hope for our future.

When we take this to heart and give it serious consideration, we become aware of its wisdom. What in this world is an absolute, never-changing, never-ending, sure possession? Any great force of nature can strip us of our possessions within moments. Our health can diminish to the point where we are unable to enjoy our earthly treasures. We can suddenly lose our livelihoods at the hands of those who have power over us, and when we come to life's end, all of our possessions, which we do dearly treasure, will be left here on earth to be dealt with at the whims and desires of others.

This is not intended to suggest that we may not enjoy the blessings God has so richly given us, but we do need to keep a proper perspective and keep in check the degree to which we value them. Things cannot give us lasting contentment and security. Advertisements would have us believe that our happiness and well-being depends on owning and using specific products. The problem is, they often fail to fulfill their claims, and even if they do, how often doesn't it happen that they either wear out, or, like children with their toys, our interests turn to other things?

As was mentioned before, nothing of this earth's goods last forever. But listen to what the book of Hebrews tells us in chapter 13:5: "Keep your lives free from the love of money and be content with what you have, because God has said, 'Never will I leave you; never will I forsake you.'" Now, that's real, never-ending, dependable security. No, it does not mean that our lives will be carefree and that we will experience no bumps in the road along the way, but it does mean we have someone who never changes, who is always the same, who will never forsake us during good or difficult times, and who will be there to uphold us. Even in times of life's storms, He will be there, giving us peace that passes all understanding and bringing us safely through them.

We see, then, that the underlying principle of this commandment to refrain from coveting is that of contentment. We have seen, too, that there are many forces in this world that tempt us into a state of discontent. There is nothing wrong in striving to improve or better our lives, but we need to control our priorities so that we do not covet that which belongs to our neighbors. To do that, we need to look at our blessings and live with gratitude for what God has given us. The apostle Paul has given us the example of pure contentment in his letter to the Philippians in 4:13: "I have learned to be content in whatever the circumstances. I know what it is to be in need and I know what it is to have plenty. I have learned the secret of being content in any and every situation, whether well-fed or hungry, whether living in plenty or in want. I can do everything in him who gives me strength." Paul had his priorities in order. That is what we, with God's help, need to do.

AFTERWORD

Are you one who may have been wondering if these Ten Commandments are relevant to those of us who live in the twenty-first century? They have just given us a good look at the heart of humanity. They have also given us a good look at the heart of God, so to speak. God's Word assures us that if we live in obedience to them, we will experience His blessings while here on this earth. But if we refuse to follow His standards for righteous living, we invite all sorts of problems and heartaches into our lives. Even though He knows we are weak, self-centered, and sinful by nature, God has made His love for us apparent by providing a way out of our dilemma.

Gratefully, He has offered hope and help to us through His only begotten Son, Jesus Christ. He alone kept these commands to love God and neighbors above all; He kept them perfectly for us. All we need do is confess our need of forgiveness through Christ, our Savior, and we will be pardoned and given eternal life through His sacrifice on our behalf. Unlike we humans, who point fingers and rain down harsh judgment on our fellow sinners, we are invited to come to Christ where we will find forgiveness, peace, and rest for our souls and an eternal home awaiting us with Christ Himself.

QUESTIONS/DISCUSSION

1. Since these commandments were given to the Israelites so long ago, are they really important to today's culture and society? Why or why not?

2. Wouldn't living according to these commands take away my freedom to enjoy life? Why or why not?

3. What would I gain by living the way the Ten Commandments require? Explain.

4. What would I lose by living the way the Ten Commandments require? Explain.

5. Why try to live according to them when I'm told I'm a sinner and can't keep them anyway? Doesn't this seem like a hopeless situation? If not, why not?

6. What do these commandments have to say about our human character?

7. Why do they tell us about the character of God?

NOTES:

NOTES:

NOTES:

Printed in the United States
by Baker & Taylor Publisher Services